Where Does the Water Go?

Mario Lucca

It has rained and the garden is wet.
Will the garden always be wet?

No. Heat from the sun will dry the garden.

Where does the water go?

The heat from the sun turns the water into a gas called **water vapor**. Water vapor goes into the air. We cannot see it, but it's there.

water vapor

When water changes from a liquid into a gas, it is called **evaporation**. The water in the garden evaporates.

The clothes have been washed and now they are wet.
Will the clothes always stay wet?

No. Hot air in the clothes dryer will dry the clothes.

Where does the water go?

The hot air in the dryer turns the water into water vapor.

water vapor

dryer vent

The water vapor goes out the dryer vent. The water in the clothes evaporates.

The water in this pan is boiling.
Will the pan stay full of water?

No. The heat from the stove will dry the pan.

Where does the water go?

The heat from the stove turns
the water into steam.
Steam is water vapor, too.
The water vapor goes into the air.
The water in the pan evaporates.

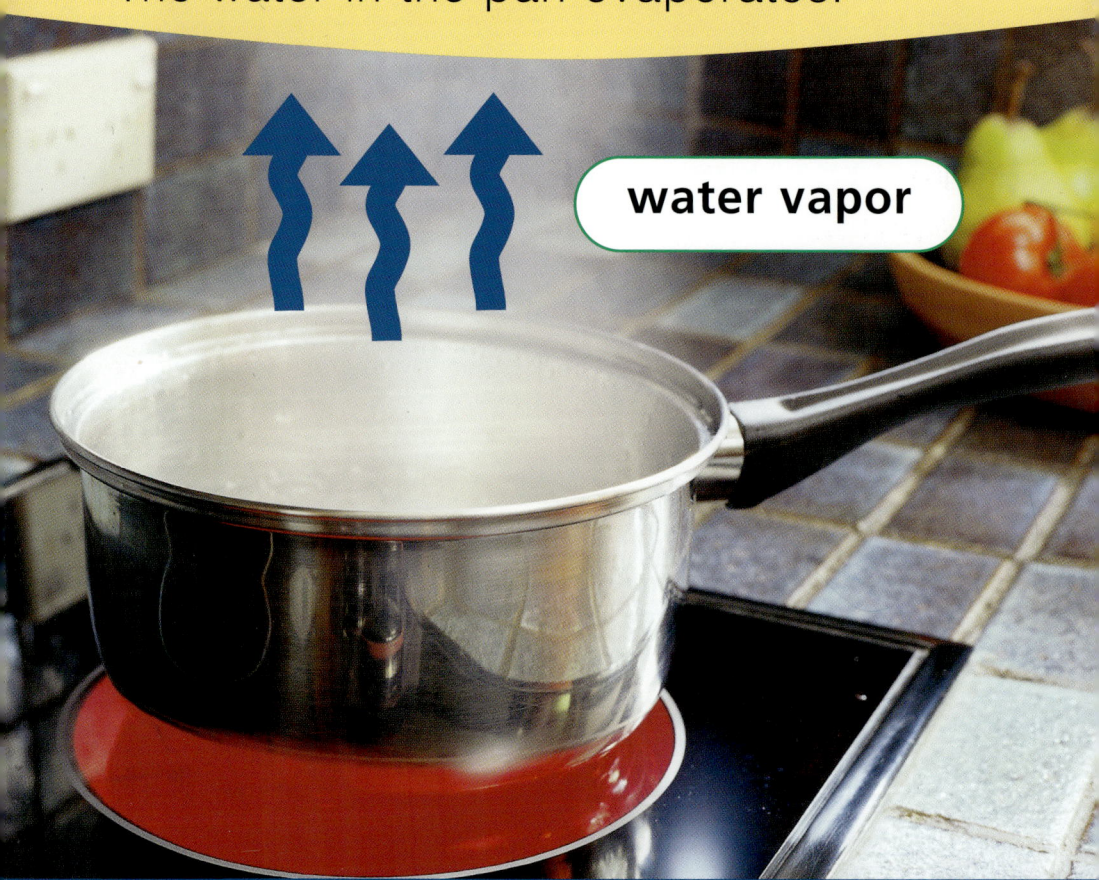

water vapor